I0504599

How to Start an Entertainment Company

ARTHUR (DUKE) MOHEAD

How to Start an Entertainment Company

Copyright

"The Journey of a thousand miles begins with one step."
-Lao Tzu

This page left intentionally blank

Table of Contents

Thanks

Thank you to my entire family, the HYLO Art and Coyote Lemon teams, everyone who contributed to this project, and everyone who supports and believes in our vision.

Dedication

To Prince Rogers Nelson Mohead, Rest in Peace...

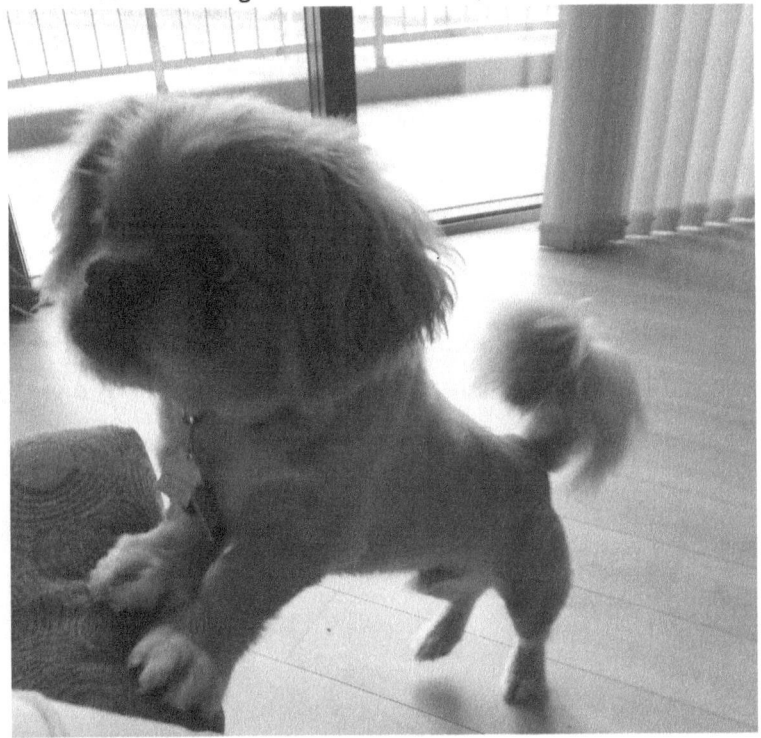

Introduction

Have you wanted to be a professional entertainer your entire life? Do you feel it calling you? Is everyone pushing you to pursue your talent?

If you've picked up this book, I'm sure you have a passion for entertainment. Maybe you're already pursuing a career in the industry, and you're just trying to get on a bigger stage. Maybe you're just curious or maybe you're like most new entertainers, and you don't know where to start. Maybe you like to read or want some advice on the subject. Whatever your reason, this book is for you. If you are ready to be a positive thinker and surround yourself with positive people, then this book is definitely for you.

Before I dive in to the ins and outs of this book, let me say thank you. In today's day and age with no shortage of information and everything at your fingertips, you chose to include this book in your process even though you didn't have to. I appreciate it! I hope this book will provide useful tips and advice for starting your own entertainment company. You've made a very important step on the path to success just by opening to this first page.

Once you become successful, others will benefit from it. Your purpose is bigger than you, so always keep that in mind. By putting others first, you become the most important part of this process, because only *you* can go after your dream and make it a success. Say this to yourself anytime you feel like giving up: "I am the most important part of the process."

Why I Wrote this Book

In September of 2019, I retired from the United States Army. About six months prior to my retirement, my 27-year-old middle son Chris, an aspiring actor, singer, rapper, filmmaker, and all around entertainer, asked me to be his manager. Little did he know his request was something I'd prayed for.

Having heard some of the dangers of the entertainment business, I worried about him. After a short discussion, I happily accepted his offer and a month later we officially started our two companies, HYLO Art Entertainment and Coyote Lemon Management. HYLO Art focuses on the performers, music, film and performances, while Coyote Lemon focuses on show bookings, paperwork, and all other aspects of the business side of things.

Over the first six months of launching our companies, I began receiving request from other performers to be their manager. These requests would come via social media, email, face-to-face, and countless other ways. I respectfully declined every request, usually saying, "I'm sorry, I can't be your manager because I'm only doing this to make sure my son doesn't get taken advantage of. But I will gladly answer any of your questions and email you what we've done so far." You see, I was keeping notes on everything we did, so emailing was easy.

Over time I realized I needed to do more. There were a lot of entertainers out there just like Chris who needed help, and I wasn't helping. Along with being a Christian, a father, and a soldier, I knew in my heart that I had to do more. I needed to help because I really wanted to, and besides, so many others had done the same for my family and me. After talking with my wife, we both realized the best way I could help was to write this book.

What This Book Is
Before I explain what this book is, I need you to ask yourself this question: *What do I want to know by the end of this book?* Okay, now that you've answered that question, simply put, this book is what four average guys did to start two successful businesses, Hylo Art Entertainment and Coyote Lemon Management, in South Carolina in less than a year. Hopefully by

telling you what we did you can avoid unnecessary spending, save valuable time, and dodge making the same mistakes we made. I will tell you what we did, how we did it, and other ways to find success in this business. I'm not saying these ways are right or wrong; I'm only letting you know some options. I recommend you do your own research and decide what's best for you.

What This Book Is Not
If you are looking for ways to cut corners, then this book is not for you. This is not a "get rich quick" scheme or a list of shortcuts. This book isn't going to tell you anything that's too good to be true. I am not endorsing, being paid by, or recommending any companies, people, or products mentioned in this book.

If you plan on doing everything for free, then this is not the book for you. If you are not ready to be a serious entrepreneur who is ready to get started in business, then this book also is not for you. This book won't solve all your problems for you, but it can be used as a guide to help you avoid mistakes.

I'm just a regular guy trying to help you start your company and achieve your entertainment goals. Please don't give up. As long as you keep at it, your hard work will pay off. I've learned over time that setting goals is one of the best ways for me to accomplish anything, and I will share more about that process in the next chapter.

One More Note

I love quotes! I really do. I always have. I've borrowed a few from friends and I've coined a few myself. My favorite quote, "It's hard being number one," is often misinterpreted. Anytime I feel like giving up, I say this quote to myself and it motivates me to keep going. Anytime I fail, I say it and try again. Anytime I achieve something, I remind myself that not only did I work hard to achieve it, but I have to work even harder to maintain it. In my previous career I regularly spoke to crowds ranging anywhere from twenty to one thousand soldiers. This was my go-to quote anytime I needed to get my point across to everyone without going into detail.

In this book I will quote some of my favorite authors as well as the Bible. I'm not trying to offend any of you or your religious beliefs, and I don't want to cause debates. I only use quotes in order to motivate you during this process.

"And the LORD answered me:

'Write the vision; make it plain on tablets, so he may run who

reads it.'"

-Habakkuk 2:2 English Standard Version (ESV)

Chapter One

Goal Setting

It Starts with You

You are the most important part of the process. Yes, you are different than anyone else, because God made you that way! You were made to take this journey. Don't listen to the naysayers, aka the "haters." Welcome to the entrepreneur game, but understand, anytime someone is trying to better himself or herself, there are going to be doubters standing on the sidelines hating. Do yourself a favor and ignore them.

One of my favorite quotes comes from the former boxer and Heavyweight Champion of the World, Muhammad Ali, who said, "I am the greatest, I said that even before I knew I was. What you are thinking is what you are becoming." With these words, Ali made me feel that in order to achieve goals you first have to believe in yourself, and before long the entire world will believe in you too. So before you take another step, please vow to believe in yourself.

Now, this can be tough, especially when times get hard. You will need some encouragement along the way, so surround yourself with positive, likeminded people who believe in you. People and words can build you up, but they can also tear you down. In the words of this unknown author's plea, "Stay away from negative people, they've got a problem for every solution." Watch the company you keep, especially the ones very close to you. If you have naysayers and pessimists on your team, get rid of them.

> *"The trouble with men (people) is not in achieving their goals (they do that); it's in establishing them."*
>
> -Earl Nightingale

Goals are Important

This fact is rarely disputed, but more importantly if you understand "why" goal setting is important you are more likely to achieve your goals. Goals should mean something to you and should be bigger than you. Why do I say that? Because it works! It's an open secret that you will accomplish your goals if they have special significance in your life and line up with your ultimate purpose. The reason it works is because goal setting inadvertently increases your desire and ability to achieve them. Trust me, if you do this your desire and passion to reach your goals will be unmatched. This is the main reason I always align my goals with my values and beliefs.

How to Set Your Goals

Some people have complicated goal-setting systems involving charts, boards, binders and computer programs. Others just write their goals on a piece of paper and draw a line through them as they are achieved. I'm not saying either of these ways is right or wrong, in fact just the opposite. They both are right because they contain the most important part—setting goals. My system is simple to some and complex to others, but it works for me.

I won't go into too much detail about my system, as it would take away from the overall purpose of this book. However, I will give an example of what I do. My goals are always in line with my core values, so in this example I have three values. They are (1) family, (2) education, and (3) selfless service. Keeping those three in mind, using these three questions, this is how I set goals.

Imagine my goal is to read two business self-help books each week in order to learn more about successfully running a small business. My questions are:

(1) Why is this goal important?

(2) Is it in line with my values and beliefs?

(3) Does this goal serve a bigger purpose?

The answers are:

(1) Family and education

(2) Family, education, and selfless service

(3) Family, education, and selfless service are all bigger than me.

In this example, this goal is in line with all of my values, so I am much more likely to not only want to achieve this goal but also to excel at it. In reality, of course, I have more than just three values, and as long as any goal I want to achieve lines up with any one of my values I set it.

Consider trying my method with three of your business goals. What are the three most important business goals you have? If you are not sure, consider starting with these three because I think they are the most achievable and will help build your confidence as you start out:

- **Goal 1: Do eight performances each month.** That breaks down to two shows per week. This was one of our goals and it was important to us because of the education we received while doing the shows.

- **Goal 2: Meet four venue owners per month.** This was important to us because of education, but it also helped us meet the people who would eventually pay us.

- **Goal 3. Volunteer once every month.** This was important because of selfless service. It helped remind

17

us that life is bigger than us.

If you use these three goals you will be off to a good start. I love my way of setting goals, so feel free to use it, or maybe you already have a much better way. Whatever you decide, I recommend as always you do what's best for you.

"Study to shew thyself approved unto God,

a workman that needeth not to be ashamed, rightly dividing

the word of truth."

-2 Timothy 2:15 King James Version (KJV)

Chapter Two

Study

Okay, now that you know what this book is about and you've set business goals, what's the next step? I recommend you study. A good way to approach this step is to write down all the questions you have and go find the answers.

What questions should you ask? Maybe you already have questions like, what entertainment problem am I solving? What talent do I have? Who is my target audience? What is my job? Or hundreds of other questions.

For us the next steps were to create a logo, find names, and legally create our companies. Those were mistakes on our part. The first thing we should have done after goal setting was found a successful mentor in the entertainment business. And then we should have asked them questions. The first question I wish we had asked was, "How are we going to get paid?" Our mentor would have told us, "This is an expensive business, so if you plan on being successful you're going to have to spend money." On the other hand if you don't want to get paid then there is no need for you to waste money or time going into or creating a business.

How Am I Going to Get Paid?

To some this is a selfish question because it's about money. However, it's one of the most important questions you can ask. Based on our business model, the more money we make the more people we can help. Hopefully you understand you will need to make money if you truly want to help others like we do. You can do like us and make assumptions based on what you think your talents, knowledge, and experience are worth, or you can do it based on facts. By asking, "How am I going to get paid," you force yourself to "know your worth" as it relates to your particular talent.

Once you find out how you're going to get paid, you can easily find your current talent worth. All you have to do is ask the people who are going to be paying you how much they are willing to pay you for what you do right now. For example, our specialty is music and film, more specifically hip-hop music and comedy skits. We get paid by doing live shows, as well as putting music and skits on our website, on streaming platforms, and on social media. In order to find out how much we should be paid, we asked people or we did research. For online payment questions we used YouTube, read books, and contacted social media sites. For live performances we contacted between 20 and 30 local venues and asked how much they would pay us to perform. After collecting the data, we spoke to our mentor to make sure we had good information. Based on his feedback, our research, and their answers, we not only learned how much we would get paid; we also learned the method by which we would be paid. Just like money, research is extremely important. I'm sure you have plenty of questions and that's why I recommend you write them down so that you will know exactly what to study.

Study Tools

By picking up this book you already understand just how important it is to study, so I don't want to spend too much time in this area, but I do want to make you aware of a few more things we did. I studied everything I had a question about and I recommend you do the same. Hopefully, by the end of this book I will have answered most of your "getting started" questions, but I'm sure I will miss things. I've asked my mentor countless questions; I've attended business conferences and watched hours and hours of YouTube.

YouTube has everything but I was able to learn a lot from reading, too. I ordered a few books online but my favorite resources were free. The first one was the local library. Most local libraries have an infinite amount of information, and if they don't they will usually find the information for you. Libraries are a great place to study, also, as most have private rooms and quiet study spaces. I studied a lot of books while preparing to start the companies and they helped me a lot. Being "book smart" is very important, but so is being "street smart." This doesn't mean you have to go walk the rough tough streets of your city; however, a good way to get better at your craft is to watch others do it in the same environment you plan to. We attended countless national and local shows. We performed in hip-hop, R&B, hard rock, and country music bars all over the city. This helped us become more "street smart" in all areas. Most of these places were free or charged very little.

Another important free resource during our beginning stages was the Small Business Association. The Small Business Association paired me with a very smart and experienced business owner. He helped me with my business plan as well as how and where to acquire small business loans. I received guidance, motivation, and feedback on all of my ideas. I met with him monthly and it was amazing.

Okay, once you've been studying for a while it's time to select a business name.

"We are braver and wiser because they existed, those strong women and strong men...
We are who we are because they were who they were.
It's wise to know where you come from, who called your name."

-Maya Angelou

Chapter Three

Business Name and Structure

What's in a Name?

When you enter the Army, the minute you arrive for basic training you start being reprogramed to change your ways of thinking. The military works hard to make you adapt to its lifestyle, but the one thing they don't mess with is your name. Matter of fact it's on the front of all your uniforms and the back of most of your hats. Everyone knows your name even if they don't know you. You're asked to say it as soon as you arrive and it's the one thing that no one can take away from you.

Both inside and outside of the military a lot of company names have meaning, and the names of our two entertainment companies are no exception. The name Coyote Lemon is a combination of my late father in law's and my oldest granddaughter's nicknames. The name HYLO is special to us and means in life we go through "highs" and "lows." At HYLO Art we take those and turn them into art. Some experts recommend you find a name that represents your business. I'm no expert, but just because others take their business name seriously doesn't mean you have to. I recommend you come up with a name that satisfies you. There are tons of ways, like name finding websites, apps, and so much more.

Today Nike is synonymous with sports, mainly shoes, not the Greek goddess of victory. And Apple's name has absolutely nothing to do with the fruit other than the valley in which it was founded. Google is an accidental name and Facebook's main focus is not faces. Once your business becomes successful, its name will be forever tied to how it's run, not what it's named.

Coming up with a name is just part of the process. Before you can use it legally you need to see if it's available. We came up with the names, started using them, and then checked to see if they were available. Thank God they both were. We checked by doing two things. First, we Googled the names to see how often they came up. Fortunately, the only time they came up on Google was under our companies' websites and social media sites. Now since our business is located in South Carolina, we also searched for the name in the state's online business database. The names were not there so we were good. You can find your state's website for free at https://www.llcuniversity.com/50-secretary-of-state-sos-business-entity-search/. The database process was not that hard and it took just a few minutes to search online.

Once we decided on the name and the type of business, we had to register our business in the state. Based on a friend's recommendation we used Swyft Filings https://www.swyftfilings.com. We were satisfied with their service; however, we could have done it ourselves for cheaper if we had known what we were doing. After we contacted the SC Secretary of State's office we realized we probably should've contacted them first. I recommend you contact your Secretary of State before paying anything.

Our Business Structures

We chose Limited Liability Company (LLC) as our legal business structure. We did a list of pros and cons during our research, and LLC was clearly the best fit for us. I recommend you do something similar before choosing a structure. Also, before signing any written agreements, consider having an attorney review them. Since LLCs are one of the most common we listed the description below.

Limited Liability Company (LLC)

According to sba.gov, "An LLC lets you take advantage of the benefits of both the corporation and partnership business structures. LLCs protect you from personal liability in most instances; your personal assets, like your vehicle, house, and savings accounts, won't be at risk in case your LLC faces bankruptcy or lawsuits. Profits and losses can get passed through to your personal income without facing corporate taxes. However, members of an LLC are considered self-employed and must pay self-employment tax contributions toward Medicare and Social Security. LLCs can have a limited life in many states. When a member joins or leaves an LLC, some states may require the LLC to be dissolved and re-formed with new membership unless there's already an agreement in place within the LLC for buying, selling, and transferring ownership. LLCs can be a good choice for medium- or higher-risk businesses, owners with significant personal assets they want to be protected, and owners who want to pay a lower tax rate than they would with a corporation."

Other Business Structures

Refer to appendix B or https://www.sba.gov/business-guide/launch-your-business/choose-business-structure to see detailed descriptions of each type of business structure available. Now that you have chosen your business name and structure, you should consider trademarks and copyrights.

"It's not what you know; it's what you can prove."

-Detective Alonzo Harris, *Training Day*

Chapter Four

Trademarks and Copyrights

Trademarks

Webster's Dictionary defines a trademark as "a symbol, word, or words legally registered or established by use as representing a company or product." If your company has a symbol, brand, or phrase, you should have it trademarked to prevent others from claiming it and using it in business. They could even make you stop using it if they own the copyright or trademark.

Like I mentioned earlier, the first thing we did when starting our businesses was create our logos. For our HYLO Art logo, we used a company based out of Atlanta called Dope Overdose Studios, because one of the owners was a family friend. It took about thirty days and the price was within our budget. We could've created it for free, but in this case I am glad we went with them, as we are completely satisfied with the logo. Once it was created we applied online with the United States Patent and Trademark Office at https://www.uspto.gov/. We completed the process ourselves and are still waiting to hear back from the USPTO on that logo.

For our Coyote Lemon logo, we used a local company based here in Columbia called Soda City Digital. We were very satisfied with the logo. This time instead of applying for the trademark ourselves we used LegalZoom.com. We felt this was a better route and it was in our budget. No matter which way you choose, there is a nonrefundable application fee whether it's approved or not. For that reason you may want to have an attorney do it if you can afford it.

Copyright

By definition a copyright is "the exclusive legal right to reproduce, publish, sell, or distribute the matter and form of something (such as a literary, musical, or artistic work)." Works actually become copyrighted as soon as you make them, but it's easier to prove if you have them copyrighted. If you have created a song, book, poem, or any written works, you may want to get them copyrighted to avoid any problems. Whenever we create works such as songs, we apply for their copyrights online at https://www.copyright.gov/. We do this because some radio stations won't play your music if it's not copyrighted. In some cases you can copyright an entire album at once, but it depends on whether only one person can take credit for all the work on the album. Just like with trademarks there is a nonrefundable fee, so you may want to hire a professional or at least make sure you understand the process before attempting to do it yourself.

"All hard work brings a profit, but mere talk leads only to poverty."

-Proverbs 14:23 New International Version (NIV)

Chapter Five

Finance

This Is an Expensive Business

There's no denying it; no matter what facet of the entertainment industry you are getting into, it's going to be expensive. Before you start, ask yourself these questions at a minimum:

(1) How am I going to make money?

(2) How much will I need for startup costs?

(3) Where will the startup money come from?

(4) What are my fixed operating costs? (Salaries, wages, taxes, insurance, rent, utilities, licenses, advertising, etc.).

There is no "get rich quick" scheme or a magic pill; you have got to do the work. Everything costs money—auditions, legal fees, drinks, cover charges, clothing, studio time, cameras, promotions, and so much more. The question I get asked most is, "What's your budget?" So I recommend you create one.

However, I don't recommend you share the actual budget with the people you're negotiating with, as they might try to gain more money from you. Luckily for me, I'm married to a financial expert. Though she doesn't have any formal finance training she has handled our family finances for over thirty years. Every single dime since the day we got married, and it's one of the best decisions we've ever made. Sure we've needed help at times, but God saw us through. She advises me often on how to handle the business money. But we decided I should handle the business finances in order to keep our personal and business finances completely separate. You should consider doing the same.

Banking

We've created company savings accounts, checking accounts, and we also have a line of credit. We used Palmetto Citizens Federal Credit Union since it's close to our home office. After working with the SC Small Business Association, we also decided to open a small business checking account at Wells Fargo. If you're planning on asking for any type of loan do your research.

At both banks our approval was based partially on personal credit, and this might be the case for you as well. In some cases the Small Business Association will guarantee up to 90% of loan repayment, but you need to contact them for help in this area at their website: https://www.sba.gov/

Track Your Spending

Spending can get out of hand. Try to stay within your budget. Learn the difference between wants and needs, and make smart spending decisions. Keep all business-related receipts. Track all business miles. We use an Excel spreadsheet to track everything—people, places, meetings, shows, everything. We also try to find things on sale, but just remember you get what you pay for. A lot of companies have holiday sales like Presidents Day, Black Friday, Cyber Monday, etc. so be on the lookout for good deals.

If you can do it yourself the right way then go for it. If you don't know what you're doing, either learn or consider hiring a Certified Public Accountant (CPA) or other professional to get you set up. This will save you money in the long run. Also, be aware your business will have to pay taxes once you start making money. At some point you will need a tax ID number (EIN). The process to create one only takes a few minutes. You can do this for free at: https://irs-ein-tax.com/?gclid=EAlaIQobChMI08GiiY-k4wIVCkgNCh0qpQwqEAAYASAAEgIQLfD_BwE.

Whatever your reason is for going into this business and making money, I recommend you figure out what to do with it before the money starts coming in. The way we do it, we set aside 1/3 for taxes, we reinvest 1/3 back into the company, and we divide the rest between charity and salary. This works for us, but do whatever works for you. Just don't feel bad about making lots of money.

God Wants You to Have Money

If He didn't He wouldn't keep telling you ways to make it. God tells us in Proverbs 10:4, *"He who has a slack hand becomes poor, but the hand of the diligent makes rich."* It's God's money, not ours; he's just allowing us to use it while on earth. God doesn't want us to be poor; he wants us to have money and he tells us how to become rich multiple times. The quote preceding this chapter was Proverbs 14:23, which tells us how to make money and how to avoid being poor.

He also wants us to help our own families. 1 Timothy 5:8 says, *"Anyone who does not provide for their relatives, and especially for their own household, has denied the faith and is worse than an unbeliever.* God wants you to help your family first, but what about others? In Acts 20:35, we are told, *"In all things I have shown you that by working hard in this way we must help the weak and remember the words of our LORD Jesus, how he himself said, 'It is more blessed to give than to receive.'"* The word says to work hard and to help family and others. And Jesus reminds us of the benefits of giving. That's how I interpret those passages.

But what if you don't want to give? 2 Corinthians 9:6-8 says, *"Remember this: whoever sows sparingly will also reap sparingly and whoever sows generously will also reap generously. Each of you should give what you have decided in your heart to give, not reluctantly or under compulsion, for God loves a cheerful giver."* Believe it or not the Bible says it's our decision what to do with the money that God blesses us with. We're supposed to decide in our heart to give or not to give. The Bible says if you are reluctant to give, don't give. It closes by saying God loves a cheerful giver. So in those passages God wants us to have money because he tells us how to get it (hard work). He also tells us to help our family and others.

Don't feel guilty about what you do with the money you've worked hard for and the LORD sees fit to bless you with. I'm recommending you help others if you truly want to, and to do it for good reasons. Matthew 6:22 says, *"So when you give to the needy, do not announce it with trumpets, as the hypocrites do in the synagogues and on the streets, to be honored by others. Truly I tell you, they have received their reward in full."*

Money Won't Make You Happy
So if the LORD is telling us the way to make money, how to

avoid poverty and how to become rich, then why do people judge what others, especially the rich, do with their own money? The truth is they shouldn't and neither should you or I. Take time to enjoy the things God has given you and the position He has put you in. Don't feel guilty about spending money on things you worked hard for. All of us have the same Bible and can do what it says if we want to. I just recommend you have balance and mind your own business when it comes to other people's money (see the bonus chapter).

There is an imaginary list of things in life that can bring sorrow, and money is somewhere on that list. Think back to a time when you didn't have to worry about money. Remember when all you had to worry about was homework, playing with siblings and friends, or going to bed early? At the end of your life you probably won't remember whether you had money. Even if you do, you will remember the family and friends more because living life with them is what makes us happy.

I've bought countless gifts for my family, but some of my fondest memories didn't come from the gifts or the money I spent. I got more joy out of watching my kids play with wrapping paper. We may not remember what happened to our old gifts, but we remember the people because they are what make us happy. Have you ever heard someone say, "I would give all the money in the world" to have one minute with a lost love one? All the money in the world won't make you happy, but loving others and using money to help others will.

"You can do it right or you can do it again."

-Don Nowlin

Chapter Six

Registration and Distribution

So far I have talked a lot about spending money. I recommended earlier that you ask yourself, "How am I going to make money?" Remember this is an expensive business, so we are not quite done spending yet. Some of the ways my companies make money are by doing shows, radio play, social media, and via streaming sites such as iTunes, Apple Music, Spotify, and others. Some sites like SoundCloud and YouTube will play your music for free. However, we chose to use a company called CD Baby to register and distribute our music to make money.

Artist Registration

Most radio stations won't play your music if you are not registered with a performance rights organization or if it's not available for download on paid streaming sites. Initially we skipped both the registration and music distribution steps because we were trying to save money, which was fine until we tried to get our songs played on the local radio stations and hit a wall. Once we discovered we couldn't get airplay, we had to backtrack and get registered. For a fee there are organizations that will license, collect, and distribute public performance royalties for songwriters and publishers. This includes when music is broadcast on the radio (terrestrial or satellite), or anywhere.

The two major organizations that do this are Broadcast Music Inc. (BMI), and the American Society of Composers, Authors, and Publishers (ASCAP). There is one other, the Society of European Stage Authors and Composers (SESAC), but it's by invitation only. We chose BMI because it was free to join. One thing to note, though, is that they take a cut of every transaction involving our music. For us there wasn't much difference between the two. ASCAP may be a better option for you depending on your needs.

Don't spend too much time in this area if you're not concerned about getting your music on the radio. There are plenty of ways to make money without being registered. Do your research and decide what's best for you. Their websites are as follows:

BMI: https://www.bmi.com/
ASCAP: https://www.ascap.com/
SESAC: https://www.sesac.com/#/. As an artist you will most likely make money by distributing your music.

Music Distribution

Some people find it more official to be able to say "available on all streaming platforms," just because it's the "in" thing to do. You should ask yourself, "Is this necessary for where I'm at in my career?" If the answer is no then skip this and come back when the answer becomes yes. If it's yes already then there are a lot of options you can look into for music distribution.

Like I mentioned earlier, we paid CD Baby to distribute our music to streaming sites such as Apple Music, Spotify and SoundCloud. We chose them based on the recommendation of a family friend who is also in the music business. So far we haven't had any issues with them and we really like their customer service. According to the CD Baby website, "Every one of our digital music partners pays differently, but the average we payout is 60 cents per song downloaded, $6.50 per full-album download, and fractions or whole cents per stream (when people listen to your song as if on a radio station but don't download or buy it)." So as you can see we don't make very much money from streams or downloads. However, it's a form of advertising and passive income for us. Our biggest form of income right now comes from shows.

CD Baby works for our needs, but there are other companies

that might be a better fit for you. Two others that we looked into are TuneCore and DistroKid. I recommend you do your own research to decide which is the best for your situation.

TuneCore: https://www.tunecore.com/
DistroKid: https://distrokid.com/
CD Baby: https://cdbaby.com/

Spin Detections

Some organizations (radio, TV, etc.) require your music to be registered with Broadcast Data System (BDS) and Media Base. BDS tracks how many times a song is played on the radio, which is also known as spin detections. It only takes a few minutes to do this. In order to register music with BDS, just send an email with the subject line "Virtual Encode" to the BDS Client Services Department at clientservices@bdsonline.com for a username and password. Once you receive the username and password by email, go to https://media.bdsrealtime.com/VE/Login.aspx and register the song or songs you want. You can cut corners and save money by skipping all or parts of the registration process, but understand this is your business and is cutting corners really what's best for you? Sometimes whether it's best or not will be based on your budget.

"It ain't who you know it's who know you."

-Curtis Green

Chapter Seven

Branding

What is Branding?

Webster's Dictionary defines branding as "the promoting of a product or service by identifying it with a particular **brand**." A **brand is defined as** "a printed mark made for similar purposes; a class of goods identified by name as the product of a single firm or manufacturer; a public image, reputation, or identity conceived of as something to be marketed or promoted."

I mentioned earlier that we didn't create either of our logos. We offered very little input for the HYLO Art logo, in fact, but we were very happy with the result. The logo is a half-sun or moon behind a cloud with the words "HYLO ART" written on the cloud. We identify with the logo for personal reasons; the sun or moon is "HY" and something we shoot for, while the clouds represent rainy days or "Los."

For Coyote Lemon, we scrapped our original logo idea and created a completely new one eight months after we started. The new logo shows a coyote standing on a hill howling at the moon. Written on the hill is the company name "Coyote

Lemon Management," along with the phrase "It's Hard Being Number One" directly under it. The reasons for the names and the slogan were explained earlier.

We want both our logos to be associated with hard work, perseverance, and respectability. We also want to be known for quality service and entertainment. Those things aren't going to happen unless we conduct ourselves in ways that support them. We always display professional conduct and appearance whether in person, by phone, or online. We are constantly branding ourselves in the way we want to be known.

Before, during, and after every show we thank God and as many people as possible, including fans, family, friends, sound techs, DJs, bartenders, hostesses, bands, bouncers, the staff, and anyone whom we come in contact with. We also gratefully take photos and sign autographs. We work hard on our films, at our shows, and in everything we do. We want our fans to know we love them and they will always receive quality treatment and entertainment from us. If it's not quality it's not HYLO. If it's not quality it's not Coyote Lemon. We are very particular with who we chose to partner with, and we make sure everyone we are associated with understands this up front.

Now, I'm not saying we are perfect or better than anyone; I'm saying branding is important to us so we eat, sleep, and live our brand. It's the imprint we want to leave on the world. Based on what we've done thus far, our customers know what to expect from our business and they seem happy with it.

What is your brand? Will you and your customers be happy? How are you going to develop and push your brand to your customers? Below are several things we did to build our brand that I hope will be an inspiration to you.

Open Mics

We've found that the open mic is one of the best and most effective ways to get your brand and name out into the world. We wear our brand during performances, we put on quality shows, and we watch our conduct. Open mics also allow us to practice our skills and hone our craft in front of real live audiences at little to no cost. They are almost always free and they come with a venue, a crowd, a live band, and a sound system. They are a great way to network and build relationships. While we are thanking everyone before, during, and after our performances, we ask their opinions on how we are doing. This allows us to get real feedback from the people who matter most, our customers. We ask everyone—security, cooks, venue owners, other artists, and anyone willing to talk to us. We get to interact with potential fans and grow our brand.

We find open mics near us through word of mouth, social media, and Google. We hit five or six every week. Sometimes we go to three or four in one night. Our original open mic goal was 100 performances in a year. We exceeded that in a little over eight months. We went from being unknown in our city to doing paid gigs around the six-month mark. It wasn't easy. My company manages actors and hip-hop artists but they don't just perform in hip-hop clubs; they've performed any and everywhere. They've performed at comedy clubs, libraries, country venues, art, and hard rock bars and all over the city. Initially, our company paid to perform at a few venues, but there are countless free open mics in our town so now we primarily use those. We've also found that if there is a house band it helps our brand more because we are known for not messing up the band's flow. This keeps everyone happy and reflects positively on our reputation.

Open mics are by far our favorite, but we can't reach everyone by doing them. This brings me to another tool we use to extend our reach outside of the city—social media.

Social Media

Shows and our social media go hand in hand. We record all our performances, whether they're paid shows or open mics. We try to edit and post them on all our social media platforms as soon as possible. We use hashtags to reach a larger audience. We've also used Google, Facebook, and Instagram ads to extend our reach. Using these sites, we've done giveaways and contests to help build our following and our brand. We don't post anything negative and we stay away from anything that will hurt the brand.

I recommend you put together a social media plan for your team. Doing or saying the wrong thing on a company social site could be very damaging to your reputation and sales, so it's important to learn good marketing/publicity skills, or hire someone who has them, and know what you want your brand to look like on social media. In the future, we plan to expand and use our website to build the brand and sell merchandise.

Website

We spend a lot of time on social media doing business. However, since we don't own the platforms we have to follow their rules and stay within their posting guidelines. You can make your own rules if you have your own website. We own both the HYLO Art and Coyote Lemon website domains; however, we haven't officially launched them yet. We felt it was more important to focus our resources on shows in the beginning. Running a successful website takes a lot of time, money, and energy, so I recommend waiting to launch one until you build your fan base and you have products such as clothing or music to offer on your site. We purchased 2-year usage of our website domains from GoDaddy (https://www.godaddy.com). We hired a local company, Soda City Digital, to host and run our website. Our website is www.hyloarts.com.

Merchandise

Based on numerous requests from our fans, we recently started selling our own products online. Since our own website isn't ready yet, we decided to use print on demand to sell merchandise, which is also called "merch." Merchandise is another way to build your brand, as well as make money. To start we are offering clothing, mainly T-shirts and hoodies. We have made a few sales but since we just started creating the merch and selling it, I won't go into depth about it because I don't know what the long-term results will be.

But there are numerous ways you can sell merch. You can go to local shops or online and have everything printed at once. This allows you to sell things at your shows. One of the drawbacks of this is you have to pay for everything up front. For that reason we chose to use "print on demand." Just like the name says, the company won't print anything until there is a demand for it. We use an online company called Redbubble. It's 100% free and you won't be charged. All we had to do was load our designs on their website. They take care of the rest—the shipping, returning, advertising, and payment. You don't have to have any inventory and the merch usually arrives in 5-7 days.

The drawback is we could be making more money if we did it ourselves, and we don't get paid until something is sold and only after Redbubble recoups their overhead. This was a great tradeoff for us, though, because it allows our name to be worldwide without us having to spend any money. It works great for us but as with anything, please do what's best for you.

In summary, short open mics, social media, and print on demand are the ways we promote our brand, but I am sure you will think of better and more creative ways to build yours. Please remember to protect your brand at all times because it's what people associate you with.

"What if I miss? What if you don't?"

-Brooklyn Buckets, *Uncle Drew*

Chapter Eight

Legal

I Am Not a Lawyer

In forming our companies, sometimes we had to do things ourselves, but I strongly recommend you speak with an attorney before doing any legal paperwork. Like the preceding quote, what happens when you make it in the entertainment industry? Everyone comes out of the woodwork and people will change. The last thing you need to be worried about is whether you did things legally.

Aside from the creation of our LLCs, we did all our own legal paperwork—and to be honest, it was confusing. We created contracts using examples we found online and had them notarized at a local UPS Store. We were smart enough to do temporary contracts. They expired after 90 days and we plan to use an attorney to create new ones. If you can afford it, have a professional do all your paperwork from the beginning. From this point forward, we will have a legal review done before we sign or agree to anything. It's important we protect our businesses in this way.

"A candle loses nothing by lighting another candle?"

-Unknown

Chapter Nine

Advice from Others

Advice from Professionals

Up to this point in the book I've given advice from my viewpoint. I wanted you to hear other viewpoints as well, so I reached out to entertainment insiders for help. This group includes professionals at all levels of the entertainment business. From Grammy-nominated artists to award-winning TV and movie directors, singers, songwriters, disk jockeys (DJs), poets, models, venue owners, to managers and bartenders. They have worked all over the world on stage, on screen, in front of, and behind the scenes.

I asked two singer-songwriters the following question: *What's the one question you want all new artists to know the answer to?* Here are their responses.

Singer-Songwriter 1: *"Artists create CULTURE. There's an art to everything. We must own, chronicle, and curate our CULTURE to preserve it. No other ethnic group should do this again in HISTORY. Ownership is the KEY!"*

Singer-Songwriter 2: *"Stay consistent and keep perfecting your craft."*

I asked other professionals the following four questions:

1. How long have you worked in that role?
2. What's the biggest mistake you see entertainers make?
3. What can entertainers do to impress the audience?
4. If you could give entertainers all over one piece of advice, what would it be?

These are their jobs and their answers.

Behind-the-Scenes Coordinator Co-Owner & Operator of a Musician/Artist Development Company:

1. *How long have you worked in that role?*
"I've worked this role for over 10 years."

2. *What's the biggest mistake you see entertainers make?*
"One of the biggest mistakes I see entertainers make is not sticking with the managers or team that help get them get to (the) limelight."

3. *What can entertainers do to impress the audience?*
"The live show is where it really counts. If the audience feels like

they got their money's worth after you perform, then they will always be impressed by the entertainer. This is where solid fan bases begin."

4. If you could give entertainers all over one piece of advice, what would it be?

"I would tell them (to) make sure the music that they give us is from the heart. As fans we can tell when it's not pure. If it's not from the heart or if the entertainer don't feel they gave 100%, then don't give it to us until it's 100."

Musician/Drummer/Producer/Songwriter:

1. How long have you worked in that role?

"Over 20 years."

2. What's the biggest mistake you see entertainers make?

"Not being themselves."

3. What can entertainers do to impress the audience?

"Give a high energetic show and perform all the songs of yours that you think they most likely came to hear."

4. If you could give entertainers all over one piece of advice, what would it be?

"Work hard and treat the people that are helping you get to

where you need to be honestly."

Artist, Poet, Photographer, Filmmaker, Author and Promoter of Performance Art Events:

1. *How long have you worked in that role?*

"I've been an artist for what feels like my entire life, but I've only begun taking things seriously with the business side of things for about 5 years now."

2. *What's the biggest mistake you see entertainers make?*

"The biggest mistake I often see entertainers make is not being patient with the process it takes to make a name for themselves. I think a lot of performers watch social media and see how quickly new artists go viral with a song, video, etc. and believe they can easily attain that same level of success overnight. So, when that doesn't happen from lack of consistency, lack of substance, or their art just not capturing the attention of the masses in this very moment, they often give up on properly promoting themselves."

3. *What can entertainers do to impress the audience?*

"The best business advice I can remember someone giving me is that consumers return to you not so much for the product you're selling, but for the experience they have while shopping with your company. If audience members don't feel a genuine connection with you as an artist, they're likely to completely forget you moments after seeing you perform. With that in mind, I feel like audience members are always the most impressed when you put in the extra effort to connect with them on a human level both on and off the stage."

4. *If you could give entertainers all over one piece of advice, what would it be?*
"Consistency is absolute key! It really does take time to attain true success in this industry in a way that gets you known and gets you paid. Distance yourself from anyone taking away from you taking control of your life and going to the next level. Make a plan, stick to it, modify when needed, but KEEP GOING no matter what. The second that little voice tells you to give up/you're not talented enough/you're not ready for this is the same second the breakthrough is finally ready to hit. And when it does, I promise it'll bring a sense of joy, pride, and accomplishment you can't even begin to describe!"

Restaurant & Bar General Manager:
1. *How long have you worked in that role?*
"Since the business opened in August 2015." (Five years.)

2. *What's the biggest mistake you see entertainers make?*
"When first starting out and they haven't developed a following

they charge too much for a performance."

3. *What can entertainers do to impress the audience?*
"Learn the audience they are performing for. Do their homework and perform the music that aligns with the audience."

4. *If you could give entertainers all over one piece of advice, what would it be?*
"Don't be afraid to hustle and grind to make your dreams come true. Sometimes performances are not always about a dollar. Sometimes there are opportunities to grow your fan base. Then the money will come. All performances are important. Perform like you mean it!!!"

DJ/Artist:
1. *How long have you worked in that role?*
"Roughly 2-3 years as (a) DJ, roughly 9 years in the music industry."

2. *What's the biggest mistake you see entertainers make?*
"Not being prepared for ANY audience; lack of effective marketing."

3. *What can entertainers do to impress the audience?*

"Cultivate the performance as a whole; give the audience something (positive) to remember about you."

4. *If you could give entertainers all over one piece of advice, what would it be?*

"Make sure you're confident in yourself first. Cultivate your craft, know it well, and present it well. Excellence doesn't have a city, state, or platform attached to it. Give excellence every time. And, everyone is not your friend NOR (are) they your enemy."

Film Production Manager/Executive Play Production Manager/Play Producer and Director:

1. *How long have you worked in that role?*

"I have worked in film and manuscript for over 20 years in some capacity."

2. *What's the biggest mistake you see entertainers make?*

"One of the biggest mistakes I have seen entertainers make is micromanagement at the upper level. It's important to put people in place based on skill and trust. It takes many parts working in excellence to achieve success. One person, no matter how talented, skillful, or experienced, cannot do everything and reach ultimate success unless you are Jesus."

3. *What can entertainers do to impress the audience?*

"The best way to impress an audience is to be 100! Be real! Be honest! Be true! If you talk the talk, walk the walk."

4. *If you could give entertainers all over one piece of advice, what would it be?*

"My advice is always make sure your reflection can fit in one mirror and check that image often. It's not enough to just remember where you came from but use that energy to catapult yourself forward and keep a lifeline available for others. Never allow ego to be your driver in life."

Model/Actress/Promoter.:

1. *How long have you worked in that role?*

"Since 2009 off and on. 2015 I made it a constant thing."

2. *What's the biggest mistake you see entertainers make?*

"Some don't show that they believe in their own work and won't spend anything in order to get their music/business promoted the right way or to be seen. Hiring the wrong manager or just jumping into a contract without understanding the contracts."

3. *What can entertainers do to impress the audience?*

"(Use) body language, handle the performance and the

audience, learn your supporters and own the show. Get the audience to participate in your performance and interact with the crowd; don't just stand like a statue."

4. *If you could give entertainers all over one piece of advice, what would it be?*
"Don't be a yes person. Turn some jobs and events down because everything is not a good look. It's not good to be a YES TO EVERYTHING PERSON."

Manager/Promoter/Sound Engineer/Songwriter:

1. *How long have you worked in that role?*
"I have always enjoyed music immensely; however, I only recently pursued it as career. I have been working in the music scene for 3 years now."

2. *What's the biggest mistake you see entertainers make?*
"Not connecting with other musicians, creatives, entrepreneurs, etc., which is in part fueled by the American Idol fantasy of being 'discovered.' To quote my favorite cadence, 'Hard Work is Hard Work!' You wouldn't buy a scratch-off tickets and call yourself a High Risk Investor! So if (you) want to succeed you have to put in the work. Surround yourself with like-minded, motivated people who understand this and want you and everyone around you to succeed."

3. What can entertainers do to impress the audience?

"Be as excited about what you are doing as you would want the audience to be before, during, and after the performance. It's perfectly acceptable to be humble but remember you've created something amazing, and you should be excited. And, if you're excited everyone else will be too."

4. If you could give entertainers all over one piece of advice, what would it be?

"This brings me back to Question #3. Remember that you can't play this game alone. You need a team, you may be the one on stage, but you a never alone. If they support your music they are on your team. Set goals for yourself. Lastly, never play for free. Charity can be written off, open mics are good way to test new sounds and express ideas to a willing audience, but if someone (asks) you to play a full set for exposure and there's less than 10k people, you're being taken advantage of. (Beer and food is not payment)."

Club Manager/Bartender:

1. How long have you worked in that role?
"Ten years."

2. What's the biggest mistake you see entertainers make?

"Not milking the moment."

3. *What can entertainers do to impress the audience?*
"Your introduction and first impression should capture the audience."

4. *If you could give entertainers all over one piece of advice, what would it be?*
"Everything ain't for everybody, but everybody loves something."

Artist/ Actor/Writer/Entrepreneur:
1. *How long have you worked in that role?*
"Ten years."

2. *What's the biggest mistake you see entertainers make?*
"Not understanding the business part of art and trusting the wrong people."

3. *What can entertainers do to impress the audience?*
"Perfect you art first then bring the crowd into your world. Be engaging."

4. *If you could give entertainers all over one piece of advice, what would it be?*

"Be smart about how you move and constantly be yourself. Only you can be you."

Comedian:

1. *How long have you worked in that role?*
"Two years."

2. *What's the biggest mistake you see entertainers make?*
"Letting negativity stop them, or getting complacent and not growing their skill set."

3. *What can entertainers do to impress the audience?*
"Properly interact with them."

4. *If you could give entertainers all over one piece of advice, what would it be?*
"Keep your imagination as crazy as possible. It makes it easier to be creative."

Comedian/Actor/Writer/Guitarist:

1. *How long have you worked in that role?*
"Two years in comedy and acting, a few months writing. I've played guitar most of my life."

2. *What's the biggest mistake you see entertainers make?*

"Procrastination."

3. *What can entertainers do to impress the audience?*
"Interact with the crowd. Feel their energy; bring them up to your level."

4. *If you could give entertainers all over one piece of advice, what would it be?*
"Positive energy allows constant elevation."

Rapper/Singer/Producer/Writer/Actor/Director:
1. *How long have you worked in that role?*
"Writing, rapping, producing 11 years. Acting and directing 3 years."

2. *What's the biggest mistake you see entertainers make?*
"Expecting to make it off of pure talent without putting in hard work."

3. *What can entertainers do to impress the audience?*
"Simply practice before you present. You'll be more confident in your work and they'll be able to feel it."

4. *If you could give entertainers all over one piece of advice, what would it be?*

"Don't try to be different. Just be true to yourself; you're already different."

Artist:

1. *How long have you worked in that role?*

"I've been rapping ever since I was 8 years old. Not being boastful, but around 13 is (when) I started to notice that my content started to surpass my peers, making them all say, 'My verse gotta be better than (mine).'"

2. *What's the biggest mistake you see entertainers make?*

"Not being original, but at the same time trying to be too genuine by catering only to one crowd. As an artist you have to grow and also change with the times. Don't lose yourself, but don't sound outdated either."

3. *What can entertainers do to impress the audience?*

"Engage with the audience. Make it personal. Play music they know about whether new or old to get them ready for you and own the stage. Confidence is key!"

4. *If you could give entertainers all over one piece of advice what would it be?*

"Stay relevant and consistent."

Bartender:

1. *How long have you worked in that role?*
"Nine years."

2. *What's the biggest mistake you see entertainers make?*
"The biggest mistake is entertainers getting (drunk)."

3. *What can entertainers do to impress the audience?*
"Be the entertainment."

4. *If you could give entertainers all over one piece of advice, what would it be?*
"Don't get sexually involved with the staff."

Radio/Club DJ:

1. *How long have you worked in that role?*
"I've been DJing for about 15 plus years and just now (I'm) getting introduced to radio after not wanting to do it for numerous years."

2. *What's the biggest mistake you see entertainers make?*
"The biggest mistake I see entertainers make is not networking with others. I say this because I see local (acts) get a hit on the radio, then they don't (advance) after that because they are not recognizing the DJs. Instead they feel the DJs owe them

something. You gotta be humble and consistent and not get big headed."

3. *What can entertainers do to impress the audience?*
"This is a GREAT QUESTION!!! I've always said entertainers need to move the crowd. If you are local you can't be stiff on stage. You gotta move around like crazy on stage because the audience gets bored easily, whereas if you ('re) moving around you got their attention."

4. *If you could give entertainers all over one piece of advice, what would it be?*
"Learn the fundamentals of the game. This industry is 90% business. It's all about who you know."

Promoter/Record Label Artists and Repertoire (A&R)/DJ:
1. *How long have you worked in that role?*
"Eleven years."

2. *What's the biggest mistake you see entertainers make?*
"Wanting a big sign on bonus, not realizing (even) if their music doesn't sell (they still have to pay the label back). They may think they're the best but it's left up to fans to say how good they (are). (It also depends) on how well they are promoted."

3. *What can entertainers do to impress the audience?*
"Sell themselves like never before, get the crowd into it, hype them up like never before, move around, perform like they did in the old days. Sing, dance, pull fans out of the crowd, look to see who has the most energy and focus on them. The others will want the same thing. I have skits set up for my artist."

4. *If you could give entertainers all over one piece of advice what would it be?*
"I don't care if only one person shows up to your show, perform like it's your last time. Give them their money's worth and let them know you are nothing without them. Pass out free things. It doesn't have to be big. Some examples are shirts, CDs, bumper stickers, or a picture with your autograph."

Musician:
1. *How long have you worked in that role?*
"Eight years."

2. *What's the biggest mistake you see entertainers make?*
"Poor preparation and lack of character."

3. *What can entertainers do to impress the audience?*
"Connect with the audience. Study audiences to know how to entertain them while staying true to yourself."

4. *If you could give entertainers all over one piece of advice, what would it be?*

"Study. Study music, study lyrics, study the greats, study your performances! Study."

Screenwriter/Editor/Acting Teacher/Coach:

1. *How long have you worked in that role?*

"I have worked professionally as a writer for 20 years. 10 years as a director. 5 years as an acting teacher/coach."

2. *What's the biggest mistake you see entertainers make?*

"The biggest mistake entertainers make is having unrealistic expectations. Everyone believes they will become rich and famous overnight when the reality is 90% (of) people in the industry are just getting by."

3. *What can entertainers do to impress the audience?*

"The best thing an entertainer can do to impress the audience is not try to impress the audience. Entertainers should be constantly striving to live their truth through their art, fully enjoying what they are doing. Live the life you love."

4. *If you could give entertainers all over one piece of advice, what would it be?*

"The life between 'action' and 'cut,' the time spent performing on stage. These are very short spans of time. 85% of what you'll be doing is working to improve your craft, becoming better at what you're doing. ENJOY THE PROCESS! Take pleasure in getting better, in practice and rehearsal. Fall in love with growing in your craft."

I hope this advice helps. Thank you once again to everyone who answered my questions.

"What has procrastination ever done for you that makes you remain so loyal to it?"

-Erin Wiley Sands

Chapter Ten

Get Started

The book is mostly about how we started our companies, but I do want to share some of the things we've done after starting. We keep God first in everything we do and it's worked great for us. American novelist Brad Thor advised us "Success leaves clues," so you may want to find someone successful to emulate. We found a great mentor as soon we started considering going into this business. He has always been more than happy to help us. He's saved us a lot of money and before we make any big decisions we contact him. Also we are not afraid to hear "no." As a matter of fact, sometimes it lets us know we are on the right track. Just trust your gut and if it feels wrong don't do it. I am never disappointed or upset when someone doesn't believe in our dream. I mean, why should I be? It's our dream, not theirs.

Shows

We keep track of all dates and locations of all our performances. We use this as part of our press kit. We also track all of our miles and meals for tax purposes.

Office

Start where you are. I have a home office to run the businesses and it's great. We started in the garage but converted one of the bedrooms into an office as things picked up.

Family

Be prepared to work. I haven't had a day off in almost a year, but I am determined to reach our goals and I love what I'm doing. We have a monthly family event just to reconnect and have fun with the entire family. My family is very supportive, and I recommend you ensure your family and significant other understand the time this business requires. We are on the road a lot and we have a lot of late nights.

Network

I completely agree with John Wooden when he said, *"The main ingredient of stardom is the rest of the team."* I learned early on in my Army days that having a great team will help you become successful. We have excellent teams at both HYLO Art and Coyote Lemon. In addition, we have a network of DJs, venue owners, promoters, bartenders, and others in the entertainment business whom we consider associates. I communicate with them at least once a week face-to-face or via a simple text or social media message. I want them to understand how important they are to our success.

Be Aware of Your Surroundings

We understand this is a job, so we take care of business as soon as we arrive. While we are out doing shows and networking we find ourselves in all types of environments so we use caution. Just like on an airplane we have a safety plan. I identify all the exits and security. We never go anywhere alone. We don't always enter together even if we rode together. We look out for each other at all times. The entire team knows exactly what to do in the event of an emergency.

Keep Learning

You should never stop learning. I wasn't an avid reader before but I am now. I make it a goal to read something educational daily. I also use YouTube to learn all the time. I try to help others by sharing interesting tips and ideas I come across.

Look and Act the Part

I dress business casual at a minimum anytime I am doing company business. Ask yourself, what message are you trying to send and is it helping the brand?

Meetings

In my opinion, you can never have too many meetings. Even

though we see each other daily, we have meetings set aside on Mondays and Fridays. I try to have open and honest conversations with everyone on the team as much as possible. What will happen when we make it? We have a plan for what to do once we achieve our goals. The plan answers questions like how to disband or sell the company, how to add and remove partners, how to retire, and other questions on how to handle our imminent success.

Just in Case

According to Will Smith, *"There is no need for plan B because plan A is going to work."* I have always believed this. As a matter of fact, this paragraph was not in the first draft of this book. This was added due to current events going on in the world, namely Coronavirus disease 2019 or COVID-19. What if every performance venue in your city has to close due to a global pandemic? Even though it's good to have faith your initial plan will work, I recommend you have backup plans in place until you can get back to plan A. We have things in place, namely my retirement pension, but now we are considering other things such as business insurance, investments, business emergency funds, and other passive income. Given the current situation with COVID-19, I wish we already had these things lined up. Hopefully by the time this book goes to print my prayers will have been answered and COVID-19 will be cured and eliminated.

Ready? Set? Get to Work!

You've finished the "how to" portion of the book, which means it's time to get started! It's time to take everything you've figured out—what you want your company to be, how you plan to make money, and what your first steps will be—and put your ideas into action.

Don't worry, you will make it—just don't quit and never give up. Don't be afraid of criticism, as it can only help you, and remember to always believe in yourself. Don't forget why you got into this business in the first place. For me, it was to help my son and others; for you, it might be a different reason.

It's going to be hard to make it in the entertainment industry, but guess what? "It's hard being number one."

"And the king shall answer and say unto them,
Verily I say unto you, Inasmuch as ye have done it unto one of
the least of these my brethren,
ye have done it unto me."

-Matthew 25:40 (KJV)

Bonus Chapter

The Parable of the Workers in the Vineyard

Focus on Your Own Business

Sometimes in business we lose sight of our roles and start focusing on what other people appear to be doing. When I find myself doing this, I refer back to this parable to remind me to mind my own business and to keep my word.

20 "For the kingdom of heaven is like a landowner who went out early in the morning to hire workers for his vineyard. *2 He agreed to pay them a denarius[a] for the day and sent them into his vineyard.*

3 "About nine in the morning he went out and saw others standing in the marketplace doing nothing. 4 He told them, 'You also go and work in my vineyard, and I will pay you whatever is right.' 5 So they went.

"He went out again about noon and about three in the afternoon and did the same thing. 6 About five in the afternoon he went out and found still others standing around. He asked

them, 'Why have you been standing here all day long doing nothing?'

[7] "'Because no one has hired us,' they answered.

"He said to them, 'You also go and work in my vineyard.'

[8] "When evening came, the owner of the vineyard said to his foreman, 'Call the workers and pay them their wages, beginning with the last ones hired and going on to the first.'

[9] "The workers who were hired about five in the afternoon came and each received a denarius. [10] So when those came who were hired first, they expected to receive more. But each one of them also received a denarius. [11] When they received it, they began to grumble against the landowner. [12] 'These who were hired last worked only one hour,' they said, 'and you have made them equal to us who have borne the burden of the work and the heat of the day.'

[13] "But he answered one of them, 'I am not being unfair to you, friend. Didn't you agree to work for a denarius? [14] Take your pay and go. I want to give the one who was hired last the same as I gave you. [15] Don't I have the right to do what I want with my own money? Or are you envious because I am

generous?'

¹⁶ "So the last will be first, and the first will be last."

-Matthew 20:1-16 NIV.

To me, the moral of the story is to focus on your own business.

About the Author

ARTHUR MOHEAD is a retired United States Army Command Sergeant Major turned business owner, as well as the founder of Coyote Lemon Management LLC and cofounder of HYLO Arts Entertainment LLC. He lives in Columbia, South Carolina with his wife Rhonda. They have three adult sons, Brandon, Christopher, and Erik; three daughters-in-law, Stephanie, Aneisa and Ashley; and four grandchildren, Wiley, Jaymie, Brandynn and Amir.

Appendix A

Websites We Used

1. Small Business Association:
   https://www.sba.gov/

2. LLC University:
   https://www.llcuniversity.com/50-secretary-of-state-sos-business-entity-search/

3. Swyft Filings: https://www.swyftfilings.com

4. U.S. Trademark Office:
   https://www.uspto.gov/trademark

5. U.S. Copyright Office:
   https://www.copyright.gov/.

6. Logo Company - Dope Overdose Studios:
   https://www.dopeoverdosestudios.us/

7. IRS EIN website (Tax ID): https://irs-ein-tax.com/?gclid=EAlaIQobChMI08GiiY-k4wIVCkgNCh0qpQwqEAAYASAAEgIQLfD_BwE

8. Artist Registration Websites:
   a. BMI: https://www.bmi.com/
   b. ASCAP: https://www.ascap.com/
   c. SESAC: https://www.sesac.com/#/.

9. Nielsen Virtual Encode Website - Broadcast

Data System (BDS):
https://media.bdsrealtime.com/VE/Login.aspx

10. Print on Demand Merch Website:
https://www.redbubble.com/explore/for-you/

11. Music Distribution Websites:
a. Tune Core: https://www.tunecore.com/
b. DISTROKID: https://distrokid.com/
c. CD Baby: https://cdbaby.com/

12. Website Domain Purchases:
a. GoDaddy: https://www.godaddy.com
b. Soda City digital: https://sodacitydigital.com/

Appendix B

Business Structures

The following information is from the U.S. Small Business Association (https://www.sba.gov/business-guide/launch-your-business/choose-business-structure), and describes the different types of business structures you can choose for your business.

Sole Proprietorship

"A sole proprietorship is easy to form and gives you complete control of your business. You're automatically considered to be a sole proprietorship if you do business activities but don't register as any other kind of business.

Sole proprietorships do not produce a separate business entity. This means your business assets and liabilities are not separate from your personal assets and liabilities. You can be held personally liable for the debts and obligations of the business. Sole proprietors are still able to get a trade name. It can also be hard to raise money because you can't sell stock, and banks are hesitant to lend to sole proprietorships.

Sole proprietorships can be a good choice for low-risk businesses and owners who want to test their business idea before forming a more formal business."

Partnership

"Partnerships are the simplest structure for two or more people to own a business together. There are two common kinds of partnerships: limited partnerships (LP) and limited liability partnerships (LLP).

Limited partnerships have only one general partner with unlimited liability, and all other partners have limited liability. The partners with limited liability also tend to have limited control over the company, which is documented in a partnership agreement. Profits are passed through to personal tax returns, and the general partner—the partner without limited liability—must also pay self-employment taxes.

Limited liability partnerships are similar to limited partnerships, but give limited liability to every owner. An LLP protects each partner from debts against the partnership, they won't be responsible for the actions of other partners.

Partnerships can be a good choice for businesses with multiple owners, professional groups (like attorneys), and groups who want to test their business idea before forming a more formal business."

Limited Liability Company (LLC)

"An LLC lets you take advantage of the benefits of both the corporation and partnership business structures.

LLCs protect you from personal liability in most instances, your personal assets—like your vehicle, house, and savings accounts—won't be at risk in case your LLC faces bankruptcy or lawsuits.

Profits and losses can get passed through to your personal income without facing corporate taxes. However, members of an LLC are considered self-employed and must pay self-employment tax contributions towards Medicare and Social Security.

LLCs can have a limited life in many states. When a member joins or leaves an LLC, some states may require the LLC to be dissolved and re-formed with new membership—unless there's already an agreement in place within the LLC for buying, selling, and transferring ownership.

LLCs can be a good choice for medium- or higher-risk businesses, owners with significant personal assets they want to be protected, and owners who want to pay a lower tax rate than they would with a corporation."

C corp
"A corporation, sometimes called a C corp, is a legal entity that's

separate from its owners. Corporations can make a profit, be taxed, and can be held legally liable.

Corporations offer the strongest protection to its owners from personal liability, but the cost to form a corporation is higher than other structures. Corporations also require more extensive record-keeping, operational processes, and reporting.

Unlike sole proprietors, partnerships, and LLCs, corporations pay income tax on their profits. In some cases, corporate profits are taxed twice—first, when the company makes a profit, and again when dividends are paid to shareholders on their personal tax returns.

Corporations have a completely independent life separate from its shareholders. If a shareholder leaves the company or sells his or her shares, the C corp can continue doing business relatively undisturbed.

Corporations have an advantage when it comes to raising capital because they can raise funds through the sale of stock, which can also be a benefit in attracting employees.

Corporations can be a good choice for medium- or higher-risk businesses, businesses that need to raise money, and businesses that plan to "go public" or eventually be sold."

S corp

"An S corporation, sometimes called an S corp, is a special type of corporation that's designed to avoid the double taxation drawback of regular C corps. S corps allow profits, and some losses, to be passed through directly to owners' personal income without ever being subject to corporate tax rates.

Not all states tax S corps equally, but most recognize them the same way the federal government does and taxes the shareholders accordingly. Some states tax S corps on profits above a specified limit and other states don't recognize the S corp election at all, simply treating the business as a C corp.

S corps must file with the IRS to get S corp status, a different process from registering with their state.

There are special limits on S corps. S corps can't have more than 100 shareholders, and all shareholders must be U.S. citizens. You'll still have to follow strict filing and operational processes of a C corp.

S corps also have an independent life, just like C corps. If a shareholder leaves the company or sells his or her shares, the S corp can continue doing business relatively undisturbed.

S corps can be a good choice for a businesses that would otherwise be a C corp, but meet the criteria to file as an S corp."

B corp

"A benefit corporation, sometimes called a B corp, is a for-profit corporation recognized by a majority of U.S. states. B corps are different from C corps in purpose, accountability, and transparency, but aren't different in how they're taxed.

B corps are driven by both mission and profit. Shareholders hold the company accountable to produce some sort of public benefit in addition to a financial profit. Some states require B corps to submit annual benefit reports that demonstrate their contribution to the public good.

There are several third-party B corp certification services, but none are required for a company to be legally considered a B corp in a state where the legal status is available."

Close Corporation

"Close corporations resemble B corps but have a less traditional corporate structure. These shed many formalities that typically govern corporations and apply to smaller companies. State rules vary, but shares are usually barred from public trading. Close corporations can be run by a small group of shareholders without a board of directors."

Nonprofit Corporation

"Nonprofit corporations are organized to do charity, education, religious, literary, or scientific work. Because their work benefits the public, nonprofits can receive tax-exempt status, meaning they don't pay state or federal taxes income taxes on any profits it makes.

Nonprofits must file with the IRS to get tax exemption, a different process from registering with their state.

Nonprofit corporations need to follow organizational rules very similar to a regular C corp. They also need to follow special rules about what they do with any profits they earn. For example, they can't distribute profits to members or political campaigns.

Nonprofits are often called 501(c) (3) corporations—a reference to the section of the Internal Revenue Code that is most commonly used to grant tax-exempt status."

Cooperative

"A cooperative is a business or organization owned by and operated for the benefit of those using its services. Profits and earnings generated by the cooperative are distributed among the members, also known as user-owners. Typically, an elected board of directors and officers run the cooperative while regular members have voting power to control the direction of the cooperative. Members can become part of the cooperative by purchasing shares, though the amount of shares they hold does not affect the weight of their vote."